Blessings After Going Through the Valley

Blessings After Going Through the Valley

Barbara Jean Wilson

XULON PRESS

Xulon Press
2301 Lucien Way #415
Maitland, FL 32751
407.339.4217
www.xulonpress.com

Blessings After Going Through The Valley
By: Barbara Jean Wilson

Printed in the United States of America.

Paperback ISBN-13: 978-1-6322-1192-7
eBook ISBN-13: 978-1-6322-1193-4

Table of Contents

〰

Foreword

I remember the first time I sat down with Barbara Jean Wilson. Our organization was scheduled to have a large event with over 600 people in attendance and I wanted her to be our keynote speaker. I recognized that she was a person who had spent a tremendous amount of time with Jesus. She carries the fragrance of Christ and out of her mouth flows praises of him. I can only imagine that if she would have walked alongside Jesus during his time on the earth, her story of faith would be listed among other heroes of the faith in Hebrews chapter 11.

There is something in this book for everyone. Barbara Jean shares her odyssey from trauma and trafficking to true identity and wholeness through Jesus Christ. I am not ashamed to say that as I read this book, I needed to take moments to wipe away my tears that threatened to obscure the pages. Not sad tears, but tears that came as I felt God's powerful presence through her words and life experiences with the living God. Her life is a luminous example of God's transforming power which is for anyone who will receive it.

It is my honor and privilege to recommend this book to you. Barbara Jean is ready to take you on a journey that will minister to your soul, as it did mine, and give you the faith that you need to take Jesus up on his promises for your life. This book is a clarion call to be all that God has created you to be.

Kay Duffield, Executive Director
Northern Virginia Human Trafficking Initiative/Reset 180

Dedication

I dedicate this book to everyone who has gone through the valley of darkness, hurt, and pain.

I pray this book blesses you with God's healing power, so you can move forward in your life as God has done for me.

"Yea though I walk through the valley of the shadow of death, I will fear no evil, for you are with me; your rod and your staff; they comfort me." Psalm 23:4 (NKJV)

Acknowledgments

To God be all the glory for the great things He has done and continues to do in my life. I thank God for His grace, mercy, and forgiveness, and for giving me the strength to go on, even when it was hard and painful. I thank Him for loving me so much and pulling me through my valley experience to be a voice for Him.

To my daughter, Tawanna, for her continued support, love, encouragement, and unselfishness in pushing me to share my life with the world. You are a joy and blessing to me, and I thank God every day for blessing me with such a gift as you. I love you deeply.

To Britten Miller, we met as friends and became sisters over fifty years ago. Thank you for all that we have shared, and for listening when I just needed to talk. Most importantly, thank you for showing me the true meaning of the word *friend*. You are loved more than you will ever know.

To Chantay Miller, thank you for trusting me to always provide you with sound advice, and for being a big sister to Tawanna. Love you.

To Marlene Martien, thank you for your love, your support, for making yourself available at the drop of a dime, and for sharing Momma with me. Love you, Sis.

To Robyn Johnson, my sister-in-Christ and dedicated prayer partner for over fifteen years, who calls faithfully every Monday morning at 10:00 a.m. to pray. No matter where God leads me on this journey, I will be waiting by the phone every Monday morning for your uphill prayer calls. I love you.

To Christine Diamond, thank you always for making yourself available to travel with me whenever your calendar permits on my speaking engagements. It does not matter the distance; you have been there for me. I love you.

To Ivy Medina, thank you for all you do to keep my website up to date and believing in me from the first day we met. I appreciate and love you.

To Marcia Caesar-Kirton, thank you for your love, support, and availability whenever there was a need for me to cry. Whether it was tears of joy or nerves, God always used you to speak to my soul. Love you.

To Walter & Karen Scott, thank you for your love and honoring me with the Big Apple Award from The WUAWSU Project, Inc.

To Pastor Dr. Raymond A. Bell, Jr., pastor of Mount Hope Baptist Church, as my teacher and spiritual leader, for pushing me beyond what I could see and encouraging me to go forth in my purpose and destiny. Love you.

To My Mount Hope Baptist Church Family, thank you for your love and prayers.

To Bill Woolf, thank you for your friendship, your support, and for trusting me to be a Board Member at Just Ask Prevention.

Introduction

B *lessings After Going Through The Valley* takes our pain, sadness, sins, and wounded souls from a place deep in the valley to the healing, strength, forgiveness, and love of God.

He pulls us out of our darkest places deep down in the valley and brings us into His marvelous light so that we can walk in our purpose and fulfill the call God has placed on our lives.

> **"See, I am doing a new thing! Now it springs up; do you not perceive it? I am making a way in the wilderness and streams in the wasteland" (Isaiah 43:19 NIV).**

CHAPTER ONE

In the Valley

H ave you ever gone through a valley experience? If you
have not, you are blessed, and I pray it is something you
never have to face. However, for those of you who have, you
know how it feels. Your valley experience could have been sick-
ness, the loss of a loved one, being laid off from work, physical
abuse, or even mental abuse. I think you get the picture.

Webster's New World College Dictionary, Fourth Edition,
defines "valley" as "a stretch of low land lying between hills
or mountains and usually having a river or stream flowing
through it."

"A stretch of low land..." is where I was in my valley experience. I was so low God could only see me. In all of my filth
and uncleanness, I lived the life of someone who did whatever
it took to survive—a life of sin. Through the grace, mercy, and
love of God, He was blessing me.

Did I deserve God's mercy? No. However, 1 Timothy 1:15-16 (NLT) tells us:

> **Christ Jesus came into the world to save sinners, and I was the worst of them all. But that is why God had mercy on me so that Christ Jesus could use me as a prime example of his great patience with even the worst sinners.**

Mercy is when we do not get what we truly deserve. If God were not merciful, we would receive the full measure of His wrath as sinful human beings.

Mercy is just the opposite of grace. While mercy is when we do not get what we deserve (God's wrath), grace is what we do understand but do not earn (because of our sins).

I was selling my body, but God's grace and mercy were blessing me. I was doing drugs, but God's grace and mercy were blessing me. I was angry with everyone and God, and yet His grace and mercy was still blessing me. I did not trust anyone, not even God, yet He again was blessing me.

There were some hideous and painful things going on in my life while I was in the valley. Some things I was ashamed of but had no control over because someone else was controlling me. Yet when the opportunity presented itself for me to take control, I did not. Maybe because I did not want to have control of what was happening. Still, God was blessing me.

In all of my mess, God forgave my transgressions. I was still in the valley doing whatever gave me satisfaction or made me forget about the awful things from my past. Some things I could not share with anyone because they would not understand and would judge me and walk away from me.

Blessed is he whose transgressions is forgiven, whose sin is covered. (Psalm 32.1 NKJV)

I felt worthless. Do not get me wrong; when I was in the presence of family, friends, and strangers, there was always a smile on my face to hide my feelings.

It reminds me of a line in the song "Tears of a Clown," written and performed by Smoky Robinson and the Miracles: *"Now if there's a smile on my face it's only there trying to fool the public, but when it comes down to fooling you now that's quite a different subject."* The "you" in my case was God. I could not fool God, who saw how wounded I was, and the sadness buried deep down inside of me.

How many of you are walking around with a smile on your face, always chipper, telling jokes, the life of the party, and yet deep down inside, you are emotionally distraught because of the pain someone has caused you? Feeling betrayed and disappointed in how your life has turned out?

The valley for me was my safe place; no one could hurt me because I was hurting myself, and it felt good. Again, God was still blessing me.

Where is your safe place? Is it drugs or alcohol? Is it "let me get them before they get me"? Even in the midst of all of that, God is still blessing you as well.

But You, O Lord, are a shield for me, my Glory, and the One who lifts up my head. (Psalm 3:3 NKJV)

My thoughts during that time were that as long as I did not hurt anyone, I was okay. No one should ever have to feel the pain I was feeling or have to cry themselves to sleep every night. However, through it all, I was never alone; God was right there with me, pouring out His blessings.

Blessed by the Lord, because He has heard the voice of my supplications! (Psalm 28:6 NKJV)

So many things ran through my mind while I was in the valley. There were negative thoughts mixed with positive ones. The negative side kept telling me that it was okay for me to do the things I was doing, such as living a lie, pretending that my life was perfect when it was not.

When I woke up in the morning, I smoked a joint before going to work to get me started. Once I arrived at work, I smoked again during the first fifteen-minute break in the morning, at lunchtime, and in the afternoon fifteen-break before getting off. Still, in the valley, God was blessing me.

Once I arrived home from work somewhere between 3:15 p.m. and 3:30 p.m., I showered, changed clothes, and became someone else—not the same person from that morning. I made stops at various clubs, drinking and getting high. The difference between what I did in the morning and what I did much later in the afternoon was not just smoking a joint, but also smoking cigarettes laced with crack or cocaine. I should be dead, but God was still blessing me.

I would arrive home long enough to shower, change clothes, make it to work and start all over again.

Besides doing the drugs and drinking, I was also what some would call a "call girl" or prostitute. There are things I did that I am not proud of, but the only thing I knew at the time, as part of my survival, was to keep a roof over my head, food on the table, and clothes on my back. I had a child to take care of. In the midst of it all, God was still blessing me while I was in the valley.

As I write this book, especially in this first chapter, many will read my story and say to themselves, "There is no way I could have or would have done any of those things." But I'm here to tell you, until you walk in someone else shoes, never judge them until you know the whole story—until you walk in someone else's shoes This is what I was taught, and it is all I knew because there was no one telling me that it is wrong. Just like me, there is something in your past no one knows about. It may not have been as bad as what I went through, but remember: no one is perfect.

But let those who have never sinned throw the first stone. (John 8:7 NLT)

Judge not that you be not judged. For with what judgment you judge, you will be judged, and with the measure you use, it will be measured back to you. And why do you look at the

> **speck in your brother's eye, but do not consider the plank in your own eye. (Matthew 7:1-3 NKJV)**

One of the things that remained constant through all of this was that God was always there. Whether or not I realized it at the time, God was protecting me in my many sins while still blessing me in the valley. He allowed no harm to overtake or destroy me.

Instead, God was saving me. He was my strength when I was weak down in the valley. What God was saving me for at that time, I did not know. My guess is God was not ready to reveal it to me yet; there was a whole lot of stuff in me that needed to be cleaned out first.

> **Never will I leave you; never will I forsake you. (Hebrews 13:5 NKJV)**

My maturity level was not where God needed it to be. The level of my faith and trust in God was too weak to be used by Him at the time. However, He never gave up on me.

It was not until I had a drug overdose that I heard God speak to me through the Holy Spirit and say, "Enough." When I heard a voice telling me "Enough," I knew it was God because the room I was in was empty; no other person was in there.

Do you hear what I am saying? I was in a room by myself, getting high, which led to the overdose, and God saw fit to save me. I knew people personally who died from doing drugs, but my life was spared.

I made a promise to God that if He saved me, I would spend the rest of my life speaking about His grace and mercy, sparing my life, and forgiving my many sins; I would give Him all the glory.

You may be saying to yourself, *how was God blessing her while still in the valley?* I will tell you how.

From the time I was sexually abused and human trafficked by my mother from ages eight to thirteen, God blessed me by protecting me from any diseases that could have come. God kept me from becoming addicted to drugs and alcohol at such an early age.

God poured out His blessings, protected my heart from being filled with hate for my mother and the abusers, and instead filled my heart with love, forgiveness, compassion, understanding, and warmth for my mother and my fellow man.

However, my path to true freedom was a long way off. I still was doing things that were harmful to me. Inside of me was an angry person who just could not understand why my world was turned upside down. Most of my early teenage years and young adult life were filled with anger. This anger controlled me for a long time, into the early stages of adult life.

The anger that raged up inside of me got me kicked out of junior school and sent to school for troubled girls, which were known back then as 600 Schools. I am not sure if those schools still exist.

This was also where I continued using drugs, drinking alcohol, and doing whatever it took to make money. Even in the midst of all of that, God was still blessing me.

No one I met knew what was going on with me or the life I was living. My family would say I was just a bad child who turned into a lousy teenager and who was going to end up with a house full of babies and amount to nothing.

However, later in my adult life, I found out that some family members did know what was happening to me and chose not to do anything about it, instead deciding to speak contrary about me.

But God!

Again, in the midst of this entire mess, God was still blessing me, but at times, I still could not see it. All I saw and felt was pain in my life, and I continued to ask why any of this had to happen to me, why my childhood was so painful, and why I had to be the one to go through it. Not that I would want anyone to go through what I went through, but still I needed to know why.

However, I do recall having a beautiful childhood until I was seven years old. There is not a lot I remember, but what I do recall were happy times.

One such time, I vividly remember one of my birthdays when I got a stuffed skunk and twenty dollars from one of my favorite uncles. I remember throwing the twenty dollars in the garbage by mistake, and crying.

The garbage was already placed outside for pick-up, and before being tossed into the garbage chute, my uncle explained to the sanitation workers what happened, and they went through the garbage and found my twenty dollars.

To this day, I am not sure why my uncle did not just give me another twenty dollars; it would have been so much easier. However, I also remember what the "*old folks*" used to say back then: "*Ain't nobody got money to be throwing away.*"

Then there was the time when I turned five; my mother was making plans for my birthday party and sent invitations to all the kids on the block. The party was going to be held in the backyard. You want to know what was funny about this birthday and the party? Unfortunately, I woke up the next morning with chickenpox—and because my birthday is at the end of July, it was hot, and I was covered in calamine lotion.

However, what I loved the most about that day was that my birthday party was not canceled. Instead, I watched all my friends and family having fun from the kitchen window, covered from head to toe in calamine lotion as everyone sang happy birthday to me and ate cake and ice cream.

There was also the time when I woke up one Christmas morning to see a bicycle with training wheels under the Christmas tree. I remember going outside with my sisters and riding it. When summer arrived, my father or my uncle took off the training wheels and asked me to get on the bike and ride it without the training wheels.

I told them I was afraid to ride it without the training wheels because I would fall and get hurt. My uncle said he would keep the bike balanced while I pedaled. I even remember seeing a puddle of water and saying, "What if I fall in the water and get my clothes wet and dirty? Mommy will be mad." Instead, she said, "Don't you let my baby get hurt," and my uncle assured my mother that he would not.

I remember when I began kindergarten at P.S. 214 in Flushing, Queens, where I was born. Back then, kindergarteners went to school for a half-day in the morning or afternoon. I went in the afternoon and walked home with my sisters, their friends, and my friends when school let out at 3:00 p.m.

I remember the class trips to the Bronx Zoo, museums, Adventure Inn, the World Fairs, picnics at Jones Beach, Rockaway Playland, and going to Astoria Pool and watching my father dive from the tallest diving board, which I thought was so amazing.

I remember when school let out for the summer at the end of June. The next week was when my father took his two-week vacation, and we headed to Swainsboro, Georgia, where both my parents and my two older sisters were born, unlike me.

We spent two weeks visiting grandparents, aunts, uncles, and cousins, having lots of fun. I always remember asking the question, "Are we there yet?" not realizing that it was a sixteen-hour drive from New York to Swainsboro, Georgia and my father did all of the driving.

All of these happy times were before my eighth birthday. There were so many more enjoyable times. The Mr. Softee ice cream truck, which came around every day; going to White Castle and sitting in the car as the waitress came out on roller skates and took your order and clipped the tray to the driver's-side window with your burgers, fries, and milkshakes on it—my father would pass them to me and my sisters in the back seat. Also, a pizza truck came on the block every Saturday evening.

However, things would soon change from happy times to pain and sorrow. I do not even recall when my parents went their separate ways, because my father was always in my life and still around. However, on this day, he did not come with us because he was living in another home.

I just remember leaving the church with my great-aunt one Sunday and seeing a car parked across the street I had never seen before. My mother was getting out of it. There was a man in the driver's seat who was not my father. My mother introduced him to me and my sisters as Mr. Bob.

There was something about him I did not like. I am not sure what it was; maybe it was how he looked at me, which made me uncomfortable. I did not want to be around him.

One thing I do know for sure is life for me would never be the same. All the happy times I remember were gone, and the abuse began; not right away, maybe a week or so after Mr. Bob came into our lives. It would be a very long time before I would be free from that traumatized childhood, a childhood once filled with love, trust, and fun. However, God was still blessing me in the valley.

When I was fifteen, I attended an event that was being hosted by my mother and her sisters at a club in Jamaica, Queens, with a live band. Everyone was dancing, drinking, and having a great time. It was also where I met my daughter's father.

We talked and danced the night away. We also exchanged telephone numbers. He called me the next day, which was Sunday, and asked if he could come over to visit; he was from the Bronx. I agreed.

He was twenty years old at the time. We talked and began seeing each other. I remember when I became pregnant and told him about it. He seemed happy in the moment.

I had my daughter Tawanna when I was 16 years old in October 1971. When she was two months old, and on Christmas Eve, her father came over for a visit. I remember him placing twenty dollars on her chest and saying he did not want to take on the responsibility of raising a child. He left.

In January of 1972, I was due to go back to school after giving birth to my daughter. However, that changed when my mother made it very clear that I needed to get on welfare or find a job to take care of my baby and myself. After all, she had a job, and she was not doing any babysitting.

There I was: a high school dropout, a teenage mother with no means of support. I refused to get on welfare.

I found a job working in a factory for minimum wage, which was not enough to feed a baby, pay a babysitter, and pay my mother fifty dollars each week to live at her home until she threw me out.

When Tawanna's father did reappear, my daughter was five years old, and that was only by accident—as God would have it, he ran into my mother on the subway in Manhattan and she gave him my telephone number and told him to give me a call.

He did, we talked, and he asked if he could stop by my apartment to see her. I said "Sure." Just as he did when she was two months old, he stopped by, talked to Tawanna for a moment, and left. We never saw him again.

In a way, my mother throwing me out was a blessing even though it was hurtful. It made me a stronger person and gave me the strength to go on. Not so much for me, but for Tawanna. She did not deserve to grow up not feeling loved and protected, and I would do whatever it take to make sure that did not happen.

You see, there was a couple by the name of Mr. and Mrs. Carter, who were friends of the family before I was born. I went to the same elementary school as their children.

The day I was thrown out of the house with my daughter and two garbage bags of our belongings, Mr. and Mrs. Carter had stopped by for a visit, which was not usual. However, on this day, I am not sure if they stopped by to see my mother or if God sent them for me.

I do recall Mrs. Carter asking me to let her and Mr. Carter take Tawanna home with them. Mrs. Carter said, "We do not want you to sign any papers giving her away; we just want to help you because you are trying very hard to take care of yourself and that child, and no one seems to care or offer to help you out."

Mrs. Carter went on to say that, I could come and visit Tawanna anytime, they wouldn't stop me, but I needed help. "And if there is anything we can do to help you get on your feet, we are here for you."

I agreed, and that day Tawanna left with them. The Carters lived in Jamaica, New York, and I lived in Corona. A dear friend's mother let me rent a room in her home and charged me $25.00 a week.

Mr. & Mrs. Carter never asked me for any money, and when I offered it to them, they told me to save my money and use it to get an apartment when I was ready. I was still working at the factory, making minimum wage, again doing drugs, and even selling my body. I hung out at various nightclubs and after hour spots and yet still made it to work each morning.

Throughout this time, I visited Tawanna when I got off from work, and on Fridays I brought her home with me to the room I rented for the weekends and took her back to the Carters on Sunday. This went on for about two months, until Mrs. Carter told me that I did not have to stop by every day or pick Tawanna up every Friday because I needed some time to myself. I always had time for myself. Even when Tawanna was with me on the weekends, I still found time to do what I was doing because my friend's mother would babysit for me, and her daughter and I would go and hang out all night long. I would go my way, she went her way, and later we would meet up and go club-hopping, meeting different men along the way.

Throughout all of what I was doing, which was not good at all and nothing to brag about, God was still blessing. There is no way I would be alive today if God were not in the midst of all of that. I was living a very wild and dangerous life. The people I was hanging around at the time were into things that should have gotten me locked up or killed. It is only by God's grace and mercy that I am still alive to talk about it.

Of course, I could not see it then. All I saw was that I did what I needed to do to take care of my child and myself.

When I think about it, many people are, like me, still alive because God pulled them out of the filth and danger they placed themselves in; just like me, some were abused, beaten, or controlled by someone else.

Sadly, some of them did not make it out. They either die by their own hands or someone else's.

God blessed me and covered me in His blood in many ways while I was in the valley. First, there were the drugs: crack, cocaine, pills of all kinds, uppers, downers, marijuana. I got high every day, yet I was still able to function in my day-to-day living. I worked on various machines in the factory impaired, and yet never got hurt; I was able to hide what I was doing from everyone who knew me. How many of you know you cannot hide from God? He knows all and sees all.

Not once did I ever get caught with drugs on me or get hurt, which was especially miraculous at some of the places where I hung out at the time. Some were known as drug havens, where people fought and got shot or stabbed and even killed. God protected me from all of that because He saw what was coming. Even when I did not or could not see it, God did.

Leaving the clubs to make money with strangers, not telling anyone where I was going, I should have turned up missing, dead or with some sort of disease, and yet none of that happened because God was with me in the valley.

Even when I was not thinking about God, He did not forget about me.

When you feel worthless, devalued, or do not know your worth, you do not care about what could happen to you or what people say or how they look at you. At that time, the only one who meant everything to me, who I was going to make sure I protected, was my daughter, Tawanna. Thank God, she was still a baby and unable to see what I was doing to myself.

Everything I did was for Tawanna—to give her a better life, and not walk out on her as her father did. Besides, I was not hurting anyone except myself, and at the time I did not care.

Even in the midst of what I was doing, I talked and prayed to God, trying to find answers as to why my life had suddenly turned upside down. What did I do wrong to deserve this punishment? This physical and mental abuse? Did I do or say something wrong in my early childhood, which for me was great until I reached age eight? If so, I could not remember. God never gave me a reason why it happened then, and even when I prayed and talked to God in my early adult life, those answers I prayed for never came.

Even when I did not understand the reasons for the suffering and pain I went through, I still looked to God and never gave up talking to Him. Even in my mess, though I did not stop doing what I was doing, God continued protecting me from all the danger I had put myself in.

God's blessings were all around me. He had plans for my life that I did not see at the time. He preserved my mind, body, and soul for a higher work He had in store for me.

God was with me through it all and saved me from drug overdose, disease, and death, whether at the hands of strangers or myself.

Even now, I think about the many men and women who never made it or received the help they needed. The ones who were so low in the valley they couldn't pull themselves up to be saved from sexual abuse, human trafficking, drugs, and alcohol abuse, or who were beaten continuously, killed, or thrown away like trash. God blessed me in the valley to live; He turned my life around in the valley late in my adult life to speak for those who are still there.

God restored me, cleaned me up, and blessed me with a better job, a great apartment that I was able to bring my daughter permanently home to, and the ability to get my GED all while I was still in the valley.

I would not want to go through what I went through again, nor would I want anyone else to go through it, which is why I share my story about the grace and mercy of God.

I prayed and asked God for the forgiveness of my many sins and transgressions, as well as for being angry with God for what happened to me in my early childhood and young adult life.

I acknowledged my sin to You and my iniquity I have not hidden; I said, I will confess all my transgressions to the Lord; and You forgave the guilt of my sin. (Psalm 32:5 NKJV)

I love the Lord because he hears and answers my prayers. Because He bends down and listens, I will pray as long as I have breath! (Psalm 116:1-2 NLT)

We all go through valleys in life. Whatever valley you are in, remember you are not alone. God is there with you.

I will never leave you nor forsake you! (Hebrews 13:5 NKJV)

CHAPTER TWO

The Climb Up

He brought me out into a spacious place; he rescued me because he delighted in me. (Psalm 18:19 NIV)

Once I repented and confessed my sins to God, He began doing a work in me to start loving myself and accepting everything that happened in my earlier life. He helped me remove the guilt, pain, fear, and shame that had me burdened down.

Even when I was in the company of friends or at a social gathering, there would be conversations on various topics about drugs, teen pregnancy, and kids who dropped out of school. They placed themselves on pedestals who thought they were so much better. I would just sit there, listen, and not say a word. However, I was saying to myself that I could never let them know the real me.

Be careful what you say or do in the presence of others, especially when it comes to tearing someone down. They may not be strong enough to take what is being said and may cause harm to themselves, because the conversation they heard or were a part of made them feel worthless.

Everything that was being said was the total opposite of the life I was now living. At this point in my life, I had gone from working in the factory to getting a job as a secretary with the Federal Aviation Administration through a six-month placement program via Manpower—not only without a high school diploma, but without a GED as well.

I was guaranteed a permanent job with the Federal Aviation Administration if I completed the placement program and passed the exam for me to get my GED within a year.

But God!

In the meantime, as I sat amongst people who were passing judgment, I wondered what their reactions would be if I told them every negative they spoke of was my life at one time, and that God had turned it all around through His grace and mercy.

That was a teaching moment for me. Instead of being mad at what I heard, I continued to listen and then began asking questions about how to help someone who may be in that kind of situation. I also learned never to speak negatively about a situation you know nothing about, because you never know who is sitting among you who was that person.

Instead, speak on how you would help them if given the opportunity. If you cannot do that, I will share this with you that I read from one of my Daily Devotions, "Put a Lid on It!"

What I have learned and continue to learn through my tests and trials is that I am not alone. Many people have gone through tremendous trials, setbacks, hurt, and pain, whether caused by themselves, someone else, a stranger, or someone they know. To move forward in your life to your purpose or destiny, you must first deal with the darkness in your life before you can see the light that is forming ahead of you.

We are to be brought into the light from darkness so that we can be the light God uses to bring others into His marvelous light. Only then can we be a witness for God, His Son, and the Holy Spirit.

Will it happen overnight? No, it will not. We must first take baby steps and deal with the problem before moving forward to where God needs us to be.

I remember attending a four-day conference in Washington, D.C., in 2003. In one of the breakout sessions I attended, there was a pastor (whose name I do not remember) speaking at this session. As I listened intently, tears began flowing down my face. I noticed that he was looking directly at me. It was as if God was speaking to me through this pastor, and his exact words were:

> *"Before you can move forward in your life, you must go back to where it stopped being good and where the pain began."*

What got me at that point is that I knew it was no one but God who needed me to hear this message.

The pastor went on to say,

> *"I will give you an example. Let's say something traumatic happened to you when you were eight years old, that is when your life stopped being good as a child and forced into adulthood."*

At that point, I lost it. I just doubled over and cried like a baby for a long time, saying to myself, "How does he know what happened to me when I was eight years old?" I did not even know him, and had never seen him before this conference.

God has a way to bring people into your life to deliver a message when the time is right, and attending that conference at that particular time was the right time for me to receive my deliverance.

While I was crying, the pastor walked over and lifted my head and said,

> *"Child of God, you must go back to that horrible time in your life and accept that it happened and understand that you were never alone during that time. God was there with you, and God is with you now. God is going to use you in a mighty way to heal and bring hope to so many suffering. But before God can do that, you must confront your past."*

I left that conference empty and drained, but I also understood what I needed to do. Just as that pastor told me, I say the same thing to you: confront your past and deal with the pain you have been holding inside you. The unforgiveness and hate you carry. Call on the name of Jesus, repent, and ask God to come into your heart and forgive you. In doing so, God—who has always loved you—will heal your hurt and begin to work on moving you into your purpose.

We may be knocked down and kicked around by life, but if we have a relationship with Jesus Christ, we will make it and not be destroyed.

Many of us are walking around with excess baggage that we need to let go of and give over to God.

For you to do that will require that you separate yourself from people for a while. It could even be family and friends. Get alone with, which is what I did. I met with and shared with my family, friends, and pastor what I was preparing to do and where I was going to get that alone time with God so I could begin the healing process without any interruptions.

It was not one-time isolation or sabbatical; there were quite a few of them, and even now once or twice a year I take a sabbatical to get away, connect with God, just be still in His presence, and study His Word or write in my journal. When my sabbatical is over, I can return fresh and renewed to be the vessel that God can use.

All God requires of us is to have faith and trust Him. He will pull you through all of that pain you are holding on to. Just give it to Him. Open up and pour out your heart to God. He knows anyway, so you might as well let it out.

God invites us into a partnership that can change us, and, through us, change the world. Because one thing is for sure: we cannot do it on our own.

Trust in the Lord with all thine heart; and lean not unto thine own understanding. In all thy ways acknowledge him, and he shall direct thy paths. (Proverbs 3:5-6 KJV)

There are times when I can be doing something, be it at work, home, in church, or even out with friends or family, and I look around, and sometimes tears will fill my eyes. I say to myself, "You have come a long way by the grace of God," and so overwhelmed and at that point, the tears just flow.

Without hesitation, everyone would ask me if I was okay, and I replied, "What you see are tears of joy," and then I will cry uncontrollably and tell them they just do not understand how good God has been to me, and I cannot thank Him enough.

Then I begin to share how good God has been to me and how He continues to pour out His blessings on me; and because they know my history, they respond, "You are so deserving of it." They remind me of how much of a blessing I have been to them. I tell them that it is God and not I. He gets all the glory.

I had gone through so much, not knowing if I would ever be free to see the light in those dark days. Darkness is a genuine problem and can lead to depression, anxiety, worries, and even suicide, which can also affect your health and well-being.

To move from those dark days I was dealing with, I spent more time in God's Word, meditating, praying, and yielding to His directions for the path I should take. Asking God to order my steps, lead me, and guide me because I could not do it on my own.

Darkness must yield to the light.

I am the light of the world; he who follows me shall not walk in darkness, but have the light of life. (John 8:12 NKJV)

God has carried me through some valleys of pain and sadness, and I continue to thank Him for the godly influence of extraordinary people He placed in my life. They prayed for me, encouraged some, and have even cried with me.

During those hard and painful times in my life, the trials and tribulations, what I gained from it was strength and deeper faith to always lean on God.

God poured into me the spirit of hope, love, and acceptance, rather than allowing me to become angry, bitter, and downcast.

Hope can only be found in God.

He enabled me to overcome fear, which I carried for a long time. That fear was holding me back from being transparent about myself and sharing how God saved me and blessed me while I was still deep down in the valley.

However, once God removed my fears, I was free to speak. The God we serve loves us beyond our faults and forgives us of our sins.

For God has not given us a spirit of fear, but of power and of love and of a sound mind. (2 Timothy 1:7 NKJV)

As I began to climb from the pit of the valley and share a little about myself, a voice kept telling me to keep speaking, do not stop. It told me I had nothing to be ashamed of; lives are being healed, people were being set free from bondage because of my voice. I let God have full control of my life.

We need to be sensitive to the nudges of the Holy Spirit. You never know when you will be someone else's miracle. We could be the one who has the answers someone is looking for. Sometimes God will bring people who need encouragement across our path in the most mysterious ways.

The more I opened up, the more God poured into me and began to set me up to speak and share my testimony.

I could not believe it. God opened up two doors via social media. I received two invitations to speak on the same day on October 8, 2011; one was for a morning show, and the other was for an evening show.

The morning show was a blog talk radio show in Miami, Florida, with Zurriane Bennett, the host of the show. I was so nervous; I almost forgot my name when asked.

During the talk, people began calling in, asking questions, sharing some of what they had suffered and endured through their tears. The callers thanked me for allowing God to use me to share my testimony.

For some of the callers, it was their first time opening up and sharing their stories and the things they had gone through and were too ashamed to speak about until they heard me share my testimony.

Whenever there is a need for you to do whatever it is that God needs you to do or say, He will prepare you for it. He will never send you anywhere unprepared.

It was then that I knew what my purpose was, and that was to do what God had called me and prepared me to do: speak. I have to admit, I was still hesitant about being one hundred percent transparent. I only shared about the abuse and human trafficking and nothing else.

That did not stop God from using me. One thing about God: when you are chosen for an assignment by Him, you will get it done no matter how long it takes, and you will not have any peace until you submit totally to Him and accept what He has called you to do.

I also realized, after speaking with some of the callers from the blog talk radio show, that what I went through was not about me, but about what God could do to help someone else. God gets all the glory.

No matter what it may be that we go through, good or bad, we must understand that it is never about us. However, there will come a time in your life when you come across someone who is going through what God has pulled you through, and God will use you to share your testimony about the grace and mercy of God being there for you during those dark and troubled days in your life and how He rescued you.

I remember having a conversation with God and telling Him that I did what He asked me to do. I shared my testimony, and that should be it.

Of course, God was not done with me yet. Remember, I said God opened two doors for me to speak on October 8, 2011; well, the second was in the evening at the Radio One Flagship Station WOL 1450AM in Maryland. I was sitting in a radio station studio with headsets on being prepared to speak to a live audience.

I was very nervous because there were people in the studio working as well as others waiting to speak after me. I never even met or saw the person who was asking me questions from the blog talk radio.

In the radio station in that particular studio, there were three other people besides me—two men and a woman. Each one, would be asking me questions. It would be my first time speaking in front of men, and I was very nervous.

That is because stepping into that studio was my first time meeting all of them. There was no preparation time, and I did not know what questions they would ask. As for the blog talk radio show, I was nervous, but comfortable because no one could see me.

Besides, throughout the various radio stations in the building, the sound rooms were also full of men. My mind was racing, and the person who arranged for the interview said, "There is no need to be nervous, just let God use you. Do not hold back, and do not focus on who is in the room. Focus on your message, which is to help others." That is what I did.

The steps of the godly are directed by the Lord. He delights in every detail of their lives. Though they stumble, they will not fall, for the Lord holds them by the hand. (Psalm 37:23-24 NLT)

CHAPTER THREE

Solid Ground

❧

I waited patiently for the Lord to help me and he turned to me and heard my cry He lifted me out of the pit of despair, out of the mud and mire. He set my feet on solid ground and steadied me as I walked along. He has given me a new song to sing, a hymn of praise to our God. Many will see what he has done and be astounded. They will put their trust in the Lord. (Psalm 40:1-3 NLT)

The more I leaned on God to lead, guide, and direct me, I began receiving more invitations to speak and share my testimony of how God was setting me free. I was learning not to look at myself in shame. I had to trust God, no matter how I felt. I had to keep going. God would give me the strength to get through it.

I was allowing victims to see through me and know they were not alone in what they were facing. They would be able to overcome any problem or situation they were facing and live a fruitful and productive life when they turned their lives over to God. But first, you must trust God and take that step of faith.

When you take the first step in faith, God will take two steps for you.

What you decide on will be done, and light will shine on your way. (Job 22:28 NIV)

The light from God continues to shine on me. On April 29, 2012, God opened another door when I received a call and an invitation from Pastor DeLishia Boykin, who was the pastor at Grant AME Church in Chislehurst, New Jersey, to speak.

As I drove up to Chislehurst from Massapponax, Virginia, I was so nervous I got lost for about an hour and could not find my way to Pastor Boykin's house, where I would be staying overnight. I called and explained my dilemma, and she told me to stay where I was. She drove to me, and I followed Pastor Boykin to her house.

The next morning I got up and prayed, asking God to have His way with me and let the Holy Spirit have full control over the entire church program, which was on sexual abuse and domestic violence, of which April was awareness month.

Before leaving the pastor's house to head over to the church, I received a call from my father wishing me well. I didn't realize at the time, my father, who lives in Flushing, was calling me from New Jersey.

Upon our arrival at the church we drove into the church parking lot, which was packed. The pastor's staff greeted us, offering coffee and water; I declined them both. First, because I was too nervous to drink anything, and second, I never eat or drink anything before I speak.

The atmosphere was very different from before. This was not blog talk or the radio station; God had sent me to a large church to share my testimony.

As we walked from the pastor's office to the sanctuary and turned to step up to the pulpit, I looked out to the congregation. I do not know what came over me, but I broke down and cried like a baby.

The first face I saw when I stepped on to the pulpit and looked out to the congregation was my father. The funny thing is that morning before leaving for church, my father had called me on my cell phone, which should have told me something because he always calls me on my home phone. I never imagined he would be in New Jersey, which meant he must have driven from Flushing, New York, very early in the morning to arrive on time before service began.

As I began looking around the congregation, I saw my daughter and her friend. I then saw one of my mentors, Rev. Carol Rogers, who lived in Manassas, Virginia, but was visiting her son and his fiancée. Rev. Rogers also led the congregation in prayer.

What God showed me on that day was just how much I was loved and appreciated by family and friends, and that they would always be there to support me—not only for that day, but also for the entire journey He has me on. He showed me that I am never alone.

Whenever I get weary or doubt tries to enter into my mind, I recall that moment at Grant AME and the faces of the people who traveled not just to hear me speak, but to let me know that distance will never come between us. I also pray and ask God for strength, because I know prayer changes things and releases the Holy Spirit's power.

May you receive more and more of God's mercy, peace, and love. (Jude 2 NLT)

As a survivor who once was a victim, the road has not always been easy for me. Sometimes I felt alone, unable to trust anyone or let anyone get close because, in the back of my mind, I questioned their motives; do they want to cause me any harm or use me to benefit their own agendas? I was always in a protective mode, refusing to let my guard down.

I held on to the pain for so long, to the point it was consuming me. I knew that to receive the healing I needed, I had to release it, and the only way I could do that was to seek counseling.

Seeking help from a counselor at the time did not work for me; they ask too many questions. What I needed was for the counselor to listen, see, and hear the pain in my voice and the tears in my eyes.

Of course, I realized later on just how wrong I was; it had nothing to do with the counselor. Instead, it had everything to do with me not trusting or letting any counselor into my space. I had built up a wall, and no counselor was going to break it down.

Do not get me wrong—there is nothing wrong with seeking a counselor to help you deal with what you may be going through. They are trained professionals who know how to handle the trauma, hurt, and pain you hold on to.

Through the entire process of healing, I realized that God is bigger than my past, anger, pain, depression, doubts, and fears.

> **Cast your burden on the Lord, and He shall sustain you; He shall never permit the righteous to be moved. (Psalm 55:22 NKJV)**

Life is messy, but God is greater than the mess. Trust Him. God's mercy is incredible. Nobody is perfect, and He knows we have all fallen short of His glory.

However, even in falling short, God has a plan for your life, just as He has for mine.

> **For I know the plans I have for you, says the Lord. They are plans for good and not for disaster, to give you a future and a hope. (Jeremiah 29:11 NLT)**

God's plan for me was opening another door to speak. This time it was an invitation from Delta Sigma Theta Sorority, Inc. Prince William County Alumnae Chapter's third annual

Rolling Out the Red Carpet book-signing event on December 1, 2012, in Woodbridge, Virginia.

There were six authors invited as well, and each author was asked to read a chapter from their book and talk a little bit about it. There were also tables set up for each author to sign books after the reading.

Each of us received a program for the event, as well as the order each author would come up to read. I kept praying and saying to myself before arriving at the event, even before looking at the program, "God, please do not make me first—make me second, third, fourth, or fifth, but not first."

God answered my prayer all right; I was last. This made me even more nervous, because the five authors before me were seasoned authors who had already written five or six books and done this before. On the other hand, this was my first book; I had never done a reading before, and it was my hope and prayer that I would not stumble over my words or start to cry.

We were asked to arrive an hour before the event began, which gave us time to introduce ourselves to each other and get further instructions from the host.

I recall telling the authors about my prayer not to make me first, and they assured me that I would be fine.

All I can say is after I finished reading my chapter without stumbling on my words, and through my tears, and then having to speak about the section I read, I received a standing ovation. God was with me the entire time.

As we each walked to our tables to prepare to sign our books, one of the other authors stopped me and said, "You know why God made you last? Because there is no way any of us could have gotten up to read after what you just read from your book. The testimony you shared was powerful, and no matter how good our chapter readings would have been, the audience would have lost focus. God needed you to share your message of hope, love, and forgiveness to all of us." At that moment, I was speechless.

That author went on to tell me, "You know this is not the end; God is going to open many more doors for you to speak. Be obedient to His call."

God continued to open more doors for me to speak. The blessings I received from God in the valley were lifting me clear out of the pit.

I no longer live in a world of darkness, shame, pain, or guilt. What helped me to reach the light God was showing me was turning to God's Word, praying, and yielding to His will. For that, God has given me beauty for ashes.

> **The Spirit of the Lord God is upon me because the Lord has me to preach good tidings to the poor; He sent me to heal the brokenhearted, to proclaim liberty to the captives, and the opening of the prison to those who are bound. To proclaim the acceptable year of the Lord, and the day of vengeance of our God; To comfort all who mourn in Zion; To give them beauty for ashes; the oil of joy for mourning,**

the garment of praise for the spirit of heaviness; that they may be called trees of righteousness. The planting of the Lord, that He may be glorified. (Isaiah 61:1-3 NKJV)

God always hears our prayers. We must yield and surrender our ways to God, who will guide us to the light. Stand firm and remember you are not alone. Your family and friends may not always be available. Some of them may be going through their own problems and not able to be there for you.

However, God is always available, and He knows what is best for His children.

Whatever burdens you may be holding onto, give them to God. You have been carrying them too long—losing sleep, making yourself sick, and trying to figure things out on your own, never finding the solution or answers you are looking for.

Pray and ask God to help you. Talk to God the way you would talk to a friend; let it all out. You will not be judged or made to feel guilty.

Call upon me in the day of trouble; I will deliver you, and you shall glorify me. (Psalm 50:15 NKJV)

CHAPTER FOUR

Pressing On

N ow that I am completely healed and free, I can move forward in the purpose for which I was chosen by God: continuing to speak as He continues to open doors for me to share my testimony.

The more I leaned on God, the deeper my faith grew, as did my obedience to what God called me to do. I still felt my nerves building up inside of me, as well as my thoughts running through my head, whenever I got a call or email inviting me to speak.

As a motivational speaker, you are told to know your audience when speaking about products and giving a presentation. I have attended many conferences and seminars where some of the people in the audiences may be looking at the speakers, while others are looking down at their phones.

When I was attending college, I will never forget what my English professor said: "Anytime you are asked to speak, you never want to lose the focus of the audience. Keep it interesting, and keep it short. The moment you begin to see members in the audience yawning, talking to each other, or looking down at their phones, those are your signals to bring your talk to a close."

However, in my case, it was not about a product or giving a presentation; instead, it was about myself. The nerves in my stomach were all over the place. The audience was not looking down at their phones, they were staring at me intently. I even saw the sorrow and tears in some of their eyes. Some actually cried the entire time I was speaking, and when I saw it, I had to look away.

I just pray and ask God to allow the Holy Spirit to take full control over what He will have me to say when I speak and God pulls stuff out of me to share—things that I had buried so far down because I forgot or I did not want to remember. I can also feel my throat lumping up and the tears flowing down my face whenever I speak, but God always pull me through.

Many times I hear myself saying "do not cry, do not cry, Lord please do not let me cry." However, it is ignored and I just continue to speak. I remember sharing that I wish I did not cry when I spoke, and I was told that it was okay to cry as was part of the healing and cleanse I needed.

> **But it is good for me to draw near to God; I have put my trust in the Lord God, that I may declare all Your works. (Psalm 73:28 NKJV)**

On June 8, 2013 I received an invitation to speak on the Sinclair Grey Online Radio Show located in Georgia. During the talk, God began to open me up to share a little more about myself—not much, but just enough to let me know that He would always be there to protect me, whatever negative things I may hear from people.

However, God also knew everything that came out of my talk on the Sinclair Grey Show would be positive.

As God continued to move in my life, it became a little easier for me to accept and embrace the God-given purpose He laid out for my life.

> **God's purpose pushes you to be better, live better, love better and give better than you would on your own. Connect, and continually re-connect with God and His purpose, and that purpose will connect you with the best of life's treasures. (SELAH Devotional – Find Your Purpose–05/15/20)**

One of the things I did was stop always questioning God and just go where He needed me to go. Besides, there were only two choices for me to make: follow God or be disobedient.

There was never any doubt in my mind that I would follow God. The problem was being very open about my past life, which was not pretty, and sharing it with the world.

By not practicing what I prayed and asked God for on a daily basis, which was to order my steps, and guide me to where He would have me go, and then not do what I was called to do said that I did not trust or have faith in God—that I was disobeying Him and not reaching my full potential.

God will never put you in a position to do something without giving you the grace and ability to do it. Trust God to equip you with what you need.

> **May He equip you with all you need for doing His will. May He produce in you through the power of Jesus Christ every good thing that is pleasing to Him. All Glory to Him for ever and ever! Amen. (Hebrews 13:21 NLT)**

Whatever strength I needed would come from God; I just had to prepare myself to move out of my comfort zone, see the bigger picture God was showing me, and not have any regrets later.

> **Each time he said, my gracious favor is all you need. My power works best in your weakness. So now I am glad to boast about my weaknesses, so that the power of Christ may work through me. (2 Corinthians 12:9 NLT)**

As I pressed on, more invitations began coming in for me to speak and share my testimony.

The following year, I received an invitation from Rev. Andra Hoxie to speak at Brookins Faith AME Church in Lanham, Maryland, on June 8, 2014.

The setting at Brookins Faith AME was a little different. Here I would be talking to bishops, pastors, and reverends from other churches beside Brookins Faith AME. The purpose was to bring awareness to the leaders of the church on topics most churches do not wish to speak on: sexual abuse and human trafficking.

When it comes to speaking about drugs, alcohol, and marital issues, the church will talk about it, but they will not talk about sexual abuse or human trafficking, which is something that needs to be done.

After I finished speaking, each of the clergy thanked me for having the courage to speak out and share my testimony, opening their eyes to the issues of sexual abuse and human trafficking that could be happening in the church and what they need to pay attention to.

Three months later, on September 25, 2014, I received an invitation to speak on Blog Talk Radio's "Personality Speaking" with host and founder Karen Ward out of Maryland. This show is designed to help you reconcile your relationships, one personality at a time. Karen Ward and her guests discuss personality-related topics on www.blogtalkradio.com.

One of the things I began to notice was that God was not only God moving me out of my comfort zone, but He was also making it so that friends I would call were not available to go with me.

This made me a bit nervous, because I was always used to having someone in the car with me to talk to as I traveled to the various speaking engagements.

Of course, my friends would remind me that I would be fine and that I was not alone because God was with me. The lesson God wanted me to learn from this was that I was never alone. As long as I kept my eyes on Him and my hands in His hands, I knew everything would be all right.

Do not get me wrong, it can be scary at times. All kinds of thoughts run through your mind, especially when you receive invitations to speak at places you have never been or when you begin to wonder how the people will welcome you once you have arrived at your location.

During those times, I remind myself to take the focus off me because it is not about me—it is about God and the message He wants me to deliver to the people.

It is a beautiful privilege to be able to share God's good news with others—His redemption, salvation, and peace.

I realize not everyone is going to like me or want to hear what I have to say, and that is okay. As long as I can reach one person who is going through something and show them what God has done for me can happen for them, too, I have done what I was asked to do.

When we are called or chosen by God for an assignment to move, to speak up about something or someone, it can be uncomfortable. You are being asked to do something you have never done before.

Think of it as applying for a new job in your field of studies. You have prior experience because it is what you have been doing, but the difference is you are now stepping up to another level in your career path; some things you will know and others things about the job you will have to learn.

Even before applying for the new position, you prayed and asked God to make it plain to you if you should apply for that new job or promotion.

God will never open a door or send you out to represent Him if He did not feel you were not ready or qualified for the assignment. Once He reveals to us to take that step, you have two choices: apply or not apply.

If you do not apply and stay where you are, than what you are saying is you do not trust God, and you have both missed receiving your blessing from God and blocked someone else's blessings by holding back.

One Sunday, while attending Sunday school, the teacher was teaching on God preparing the way for us to step out on faith and follow the path He has already laid out for us. The teacher went on to say that God would never send us anywhere to do His work if we were not ready and prepared.

God is telling us that the path has already been set; all we need to do is just walk in it, and whatever we need will be waiting for us when we arrive at our destination.

Life is like that. You never know if you can do a certain thing if you do not try. It is better to have tried and failed than never to have tried at all.

Having faith and putting your trust in God will always have a positive outcome, even if you do not see it. God is a God who never makes a mistake.

In my daily prayers, one of the things I pray and ask God for is to open more doors for me to share my testimony. Wherever You send me, God, I will go to speak about Your grace and mercy.

Always be open to God.

When I receive an invitation to speak and where it will take place, not only am I being taken out of my comfort zone—God reminds me of my prayers to Him, and I go.

On June 6, 2015, I received an invitation to speak at the Martin County Women's Council of Williamston, North Carolina, by Rev. Cynthia Pointe, pastor at Mount Shiloh Missionary Baptist Church, I accepted.

God would genuinely put me to the test. First, I never met Rev. Pointe. She heard about me and my testimony from one of my co-workers. Second, I never heard of Williamston, North Carolina I'd never been there and was driving there by myself.

I packed up my car, got my driving directions from MapQuest, and off I went. I placed a CD in my CD player, stopped for gas, made my way to 95S, and continued on my drive. It became clear after a while that I was lost when I saw the sign that said Winston Salem; my sense of direction is not good at all.

I continued driving until I could see a sign for gas or a 7-Eleven, at which point I would exit and get the correct directions. MapQuest directions were wrong, and I do not use GPS or WAZE because they talk too much and would be a distraction for me. I was already nervous and did not need a voice recording telling me I have gone too far and recalculating.

Anyway, once I arrived in Williamston, North Carolina, I checked into the hotel and called Rev. Pointe to let her know I had arrived. She picked me up from the hotel, and we went to dinner at a place called The Hitching Post. Let me tell you something: the food was out of this world. Talk about that good old way-down-deep in the country soul food. If you ever travel to Williamston, NC, you must stop by and try it. It is right off of the Williamston, NC exit on 95S.

While we were eating, several people stopped by our table, including the mayor, introduced themselves, welcomed me to their town, and looked forward to hearing me speak the next day.

After dinner, Rev. Pointe drove me back to my hotel. By the time I got up to my room, Rev. Pointe called me and asked me to meet her in front of the hotel with my luggage; she would explain why when I came down.

It seems that while we were talking at the restaurant, I shared with her how God has been blessing me once I released my fears and began speaking. One of the things I shared was my prayer to God and how He answered my prayer.

The prayer I prayed, which God answered, was if it was His will to bless me with a home one day, to please bless me with a home that was large and with lots of rooms where family and friends could stay whenever they came for a visit or were driving through and not have to stay at a hotel or motel. Rev. Pointe said while she was listening to me, it convicted her, and that is the reason why she asked me to come back down with my luggage. She invited me to stay at her home with her, her husband, son, and grandson.

Let me tell you—from the front and back of Rev. Pointe's home, I could feel God's presence. You could feel the warmth and love all over this home.

The room Rev. Pointe led me to where I would be sleeping was the place she usually meditated in, and you could feel the Holy Spirit in there. Never had I felt anything like this before. We talked for a while, and then Rev. Pointe left the room, and for most of the night, I sat on the bed, looking around the room at the many statutes and Scriptures written on various pillows and plaques hanging on the walls. I also talked to God.

It became apparent for me at that moment that I just had to be available to go wherever God sent me; He would take care of the rest. I laid down and slept like a baby.

The next morning when we arrived at the E.J. Hayes Alumni Building in Williamston, where I would be speaking, I was received with such a warm welcome and open arms by everyone. Once I finished speaking, I went over to the table set up for me where I sat to autograph books and continue answering questions from the people who came out to hear me speak. After I had finished signing books, we went back to the Hitching Post for dinner and then back to Rev. Pointe's home where I stayed another night before heading back to Virginia the following morning.

When we arrived at Rev. Point's home, she presented me with a large, lovely basin filled to the top, wrapped in cellophane paper, and tied with a ribbon. I did not open the basket until I arrived home, and when I took the cellophane paper off and began looking inside the basin, there were so many goodies in it.

There were several plaques with Scriptures and words of wisdom written on them; scented candles, a cross, travel-sized hand lotion, sanitizers, and peppermints.

One of the plaques had these words of wisdom written on it:

Let Your Dreams Be Bigger Than Your Fears
And Your Actions Louder Than Your Words

Rev. Pointe also placed two books in the basin, *The Butterfly Effect – How Your Life Matters* by Andy Andrew and *My Beautiful Broken Shell- Words of Hope to Refresh the Soul* by Carol Hamblet Adams. I recommend both books. You will learn a lot about yourself.

In the book *The Butterfly Effect*, Rev. Point wrote my name above the sentence on page 102, which ends on page 109, and it reads:

"There are generations yet unborn whose very lives will be shifted and shaped by the moves you

make and the actions you take today. In addition, tomorrow. And the next day. And the next.

Every single thing you do MATTERS.

You have been creative as one of a kind. On the planet Earth, there has never been one like you... and there never will be again. Your spirit, your thoughts and feelings, your ability to reason and act all exist in no one else. The rarities that make you special are no mere accident or quirk of fate.

You have been creative in order that you might make a difference.

You have within you the power to change the world, no that your actions cannot be hoarded, saved for later, or used selectively.

By your hands millions billions – of lives will be altered, caught up in a chain of events begun by you this day. The very beating of your heart has meaning and purpose. Your action have value far greater than silver or gold.

Your life...

And what you do with it today...

MATTERS FOREVER."

After I finished reading the book, I cried like a baby. You see, I received the gift basket on June 16, 2015, but it was not until July 31, 2015, while on vacation, sitting poolside in a lounge chair in Oahu, Hawaii, that I finally read them. I took both books with me so I would have something to read while on the plane, which did not happen.

The day after arriving in Hawaii, with nothing planned due to the flight being eleven hours, all I wanted to do was relax because the rest of the week was going to be busy.

God chose the time and place for me to read both books, in solitude, because there was no one else at the pool during the time I was there. God needed me to reflect on the message that I read on the pages Rev. Pointe had written my name upon. God was reminding me that He created me for such a time as this, and I am just to walk in it.

Also in the basin, wrapped separately in tissue paper, were four porcelain crosses with the words **Be Kind**, **Be Grateful**, **Be Happy,** and **Be Humble**. This is an excellent reminder for us to remember how to treat one another.

Written in the book *My Beautiful Broken Shell* by Carol Hamblet Adams are these words I try to live by: "**Let me not destroy the beauty of today by grieving over yesterday... or worrying about tomorrow.**"

> **So don't worry about tomorrow, for tomorrow will bring its own worries... (Matthew 6:34 NLT)**

When we are overcome with worries and concerns, we can trust that God will still our fears.

God has so much for you; even though you may not be exactly where you want to be, you can keep pressing on and thank God that you are on the right track.

> Not that I have already attained, or am already perfected; but I press on, that I may lay hold of that for which Christ Jesus has also laid hold of me. Brethren, I do not count myself to have apprehended; but one thing I do, forgetting those things which are behind and reaching forward to those things which are ahead. I press toward the goal for the prize of the upward call of God in Christ Jesus. (Philippians 3:13-14 NKJV)

> I can do all things through Christ which strengtheneth me. (Philippians 4:13 KJV)

Because our hope is in Christ, however, we can let go of our past guilt and look forward to what God will help us become. Do not dwell on your past. Instead, grow closer to God now, know that you are forgiven, and press on to a life of faith and obedience.

CHAPTER FIVE

Strength to Continue the Journey

Traveling from one place to another by car, plane, or train can be tiring and draining. For me, the best mode of transportation, if I had my way, would be by train or airplane. Here I could just sit back, relax, read a book, sleep, or get up and walk to the dining car on the train or stretch my legs walking down the aisle on an airplane. Besides, I never have to worry about keeping my eyes focused on the road.

Another reason I would rather take a train or airplane is that I hate driving. Being born and raised in New York City, public transportation ran twenty-four hours a day, or you could always hop in a taxi—there was never a need to drive or own a car.

However, once I relocated to Virginia, I did not have a choice; you have to drive everywhere—and I mean *everywhere*—and you must be alert at all times because there are a lot of people who text while driving. Your focus has to be on the drivers in the left lane, right lane, in front of you, and behind you. Lord knows it can be nerve-wracking.

There is also the speed limit that you must maintain, and sometimes Bella (my car) has a mind of her own when it comes to speed, and I have to remind her that she is going a little too fast and must slow down. Then other cars are speeding past me.

Then you have your suburb driving, which is very different from the expressway driving. You still have to be focused, but this time you hope a driver does not run through the red light or come to a full stop if a swan and her little ones are crossing the street, because in Virginia, it is against the laws to hit swans and their young; you could end up with a ticket. You also have to worry about someone running the stop sign, so you must always be alert.

No matter the direction or mode of transportation I must use, God is with me on my journey.

We can make our plans, but the Lord determines our steps. (Proverbs 16:9 NLT)

This next journey took me on the road to speak at a 3-day women's retreat in Lancaster, Pennsylvania, hosted by Faith Assembly of Christ Church on July 16, 2015.

We stayed at the DoubleTree Resort by Hilton. There were several other speakers besides myself, and the retreat's theme was "Simplify Unclutter Your Soul!" and their Scripture reference was from 2 Timothy 1:7 NKJV:

For God has not given us a spirit of fear, but of power, and love, and a sound mind.

Mother Nancy Way, the first lady of Faith Assembly, greeted us with these words:

> *"This will be a time for us to withdraw from exhausted, overwhelmed, over-scheduled, anxious, isolated, dissatisfied, and broken lives to a place of solitude, safety, love, trust, and support as you find wholeness.*
>
> *Once this is done, you can regain strength for your next journey through prayer, meditation, study, fellowship, laughter, and tears."*

I gained so much from attending this women's retreat not just as a speaker, but also as a participant attending the various workshop sessions. There was a lot that needed to be "uncluttered" from my soul as well.

I am not sure how it is with other motivational speakers when they are asked to speak, especially when it comes to a spiritual retreat. Some of the speakers began by sharing their testimonies, and as you listen to them you say to yourself, "I am not the only one going through a dark moment in my life, or who has gone through and come out on the other side."

These women are ministers, doctors, wives, and daughters who all hold prestigious positions within their organizations and churches; they are members of sororities and sit on boards. Some of them even have Ph.D., MD, and Esq. behind their names, and yet when I am sitting in the audience and listening, I realize they are like me.

There was no pretending to be something they were not; these women poured out their souls and shared the pain they once carried until God healed them and set them free. I made it through and gained my strength with God's help and that of the strong women He placed in my life.

I am so grateful to God for selecting the special women who have been on this journey with me for so long; women who continue to push me beyond my limits and remind me that I can do anything.

How many of you are walking around with a soul so cluttered it is blocking you from reaching the blessings God has for you? You will not have peace until you come to terms with whatever that may be in your life.

Seek God to help you with the broken pieces in your lives, to remove the exhaustion of being tired of holding onto something you are trying to fix on your own. Like me, maybe it is time for you to get away and get alone with God so He can speak to you and show you that He can do what you cannot do on your own.

Find your peace in God. Get away from all the noise and interruptions in your life—the distractions, your job, family, and friends—so that God can cleanse you from the hurt and pain you have been carrying for so long.

I carried my pain and shame around for thirty-nine years before I finally fell to my knees, threw my hands up to God, and poured out my heart and soul to Him. Once I was able to do that, God had full control of me, and the cleansing in me began.

In order for me to hear from God, however, I had to go into isolation and keep away from everyone and everything that would hinder me from hearing from God and finding out what He was doing to me and preparing for me.

Once my cleanse was completed, God released me back into society with a clear mind, and my soul was uncluttered to do the work that God had anointed me to do.

Just like me, God has placed an anointing on your life as well. He wants to use you for an assignment that only you can do. Free yourself so God can begin the work in you.

Even if you cannot afford to get away, reserve a room in a hotel for one night, or lock yourself in your home or apartment. Turn the television off, light some soothing scented candles, play some gospel music to put you in a worship mode, get your Bible, grab your journal, and begin to let God in. Allow Him to speak to your spirit.

Your mind should be free from anything and everything that you did at the office (if you work); if you are a stay at home mom, do not focus on the kids, husband, dishes, laundry, or dusting. It will all be there when you return from your solo retreat and spend time with God.

When you do not believe you can do it, think that there is someone more powerful who has the strength to equip you to reach your desired dream or goal. Not on our power alone, by any means.

When you place your hands in God's hands, He takes over and walks you through. Ignore all of the negative voices you hear and go forward in the hands of God.

At a retreat I was attending, I was given a 3x5 card with the following listed on it:

"Forgive Yourself. You are not Perfect.

Show Yourself Grace; You are Still Learning.

Show Yourself Patience; You are on a Journey."

—*Author unknown*

We should all follow these instructions for our lives.

The Holy Spirit reminds me that as long as I obey God and follow Him on the journey He has prepared for me, everything will be all right. Nothing is too hard for God. Life is the journey we are on until we reach our destination in and with Jesus Christ.

When there is a call on your life and you finally accept it, you are so much more at peace because you know God has chosen you. However, you must remain humbled and realize it is not about you, but all about God. You are the servant God has called for a particular journey that no one else can do.

He knows who I am and has handpicked me as a vessel of favor. God has equipped me to do His will.

When God chooses whom to bless, it has nothing to do with merit, social status, or economic viability. God is after your heart and your faith.

He will take care of me, work things out for my good, and get me to the place I need to be

Therefore, I must follow God and His plan for my life and not be afraid. I must look to God, stand on His Word, and recall His goodness.

For God has not given us a spirit of fear; but of power and of love, and of a sound mind. (2 Timothy 1:7 NKJV)

As I continued on this journey from God, I received an invitation to speak at a prayer retreat breakfast from Rev. Andra Hoxie, pastor of Faith AME Mission of Woodbridge, VA, on October 24, 2015, and what a blessing it was for myself and all of the women in attendance. We all left the prayer breakfast having left our prayers at the altar for God to work out in His time, rather than ours. We each waited patiently for his answers. One of the things I have learned is you cannot rush God.

Besides, know that praying for something does not mean God will give you the answer you are hoping for; just know that God never makes a mistake. He alone can fulfill your desires or change them to match His will for your life.

No matter what you pray for or desire, you can trust Him, whether His answer is "No" or "Yes."

...and this same God who takes care of me will supply all your needs from His glorious riches, which have been given to us in Christ Jesus. (Philippians 4:19 NLT)

Life will still throw its various demands at us, but Jesus will provide for us. God can do anything in our lives because His grace is sufficient.

When we have faith in God's power to move in our lives, we can walk by faith over the mountains and through the valleys, and our victories will be found in the joy of the Lord and His promise to be faithful to us.

Sometimes our days will be filled with some impossible situations, but God calls us to stand firm and remember that faith will keep us at peace when we doubt. Faith will be our companion in the storms of life. Faith will lead us to the right path when we are lost. Faith will keep us strong when the odds are against us. Faith will bring us the victory in every situation.

Faith is believing what God says rather than what you see.

The amount of faith is not as important as the right kind of faith, and that is faith in our all-powerful God.

O my people, trust in Him at all times; pour out your heart to Him, for God is our refuge. (Psalm 62:8 NLT)

Therefore, stand firm and believe.

For nothing is impossible with God. (Luke 1:37 NLT)

CHAPTER SIX

Fulfill the Vision

❧

**"Write the vision and make it plain."
(Habakkuk 2:2 NKJV)**

When your dream comes from God, and you commit yourself to it, it will surely be fulfilled. You will stumble, be stretched to new limits, and may have to crawl to the finish line, but you will make it. You will get to where God needs you to be.

For me it was an invitation from Getrude Matshe, a renowned author and inspirational speaker from New Zealand. We met via email and in person for the first time at the conference where she was also the host to speak at a three-day Women Economic Forum, which was being held from May 21-23, 2017, in Albuquerque, New Mexico.

What a blessing it was to finally meet Ms. Matshe, as well as the other women and men from around the world gathered at the University of New Mexico to share their wisdom and testimonies and pour into each other who and what kept them going. For some, it was Buddha and Allah. However, for me, I give all glory to God.

While speaking, I broke down and cried, never stopping to breathe while I spoke. I just kept on sharing my testimony and being transparent. The love I received from each one of them will be with me for a lifetime.

One of the speakers I met and had a conversation with told me he was born and raised in Fredericksburg, Virginia, and both his mother and sister still lived there, and that he visited them at least twice a year.

We have connected and remained friends, and when he comes to town, we meet up for lunch. We also stay connected via social media.

There are other men and women from the conference I have remained in contact with since that time in Albuquerque.

What I have learned by continuing to follow God is that He has placed people in my life—whether for a moment, a season, or a lifetime—to get me to where He is leading me to deliver my testimony of faith, hope, love, and forgiveness.

Before I was even formed in my mother's womb, God was preparing me for such a time as this.

I knew you before I formed you in your mother's womb. Before you were born I set you

apart and appointed you as my prophet to the nations. (Jeremiah 1:5 NLT)

From deep down in the valley to where I am now, God continues to use me and my voice to spread His Word and my testimony to all the nations.

At the time, I did not know that by sending me to speak at the conference in Albuquerque, God was connecting me to people who would be part of my next journey and the vision. He assigned them to me. God showed me many years ago.

The vision He showed me one night in my dream would come to pass years later, though at the time I did not understand what God was trying to tell me.

One Saturday night fourteen years ago, what I thought was a dream was God's real vision. My eyes were opened, but I could not move. There was a bright light in my bedroom, and the top sheet on my bed was moving up and down.

The funny thing is I was not afraid. Usually, I sleep on my stomach, facing the wall with the bedroom door closed.

While I laid in bed, I could feel my head being turned towards the door, which was now opened. A light was on. Mind you, and I was still in sleep mode.

However, I could feel myself getting out of bed and walking towards the light. As I turned, I looked down the stairs in my house, and the whole first floor was beaming with light. What

I saw were many people from all over the world sitting on a grassy field, looking up intently at someone speaking.

Curious, I asked, "Who are they looking at?" I could feel my head being lifted, and was surprised to see the crowd was watching me.

My first thought was *they are listening to me speak*, but how could that be when I did not even speak their languages? At one point, I woke up, looked around the bedroom, felt a warm sensation go through my body, and went back to sleep.

The next morning when I woke up, I was excited and could not wait to get to church to share the vision with my former pastor at that time.

Arriving at church, I shared with him and another pastor who was visiting, as well as the guest speaker, what happened to me the night before. While sharing my vision, the visiting pastor walked away for a moment and returned with his Bible, which he had opened to the Book of Acts Chapter 10:9-15. He began reading it to me and my former pastor.

After the pastor finished reading the Scripture, he asked me if I understood what God was saying to Peter:

> **And a voice came to him, "Rise, Peter; kill and eat." But Peter said, "Not so Lord! For I have never eaten anything uncommon or unclean." And a voice spoke to him again the second time, "What God has cleansed you must not call common. (Acts 10:13-15 NKJV)**

The pastor went on to explain to me that God was enlarging my territory to speak to every nation and in every language. When the time comes for God to send me, all I need to do is open my mouth, and God will speak through me; the people would understand. I was reminded of the prayer of Jabez when He asked God to enlarge his territory.

> **And Jabez called on the God of Israel saying, Oh that you would bless me indeed, and enlarge my territory, that Your hand would be with me, and that You would keep me from evil, that I may not cause pain! So God granted him what he request. (1 Chronicles 4:10 NKJV)**

All of this was revealed to me in 2003. As I continued to move forward in my life, I never forgot the vision revealed to me. I have to admit, I never thought sharing my testimony would take me out of my comfort zone.

However, in 2017 that vision came to pass when I received a call from Getrude Matshe with an invitation to join her in New York and speak at the United Nations. Remember, I met Ms. Matshe for the first time in Albuquerque, New Mexico.

People would attend from all over the world who did not speak my language. However, I remember what the guest pastor had said to me all those years ago: all I'd have to do is open my mouth, and God would speak through me, which is what God did. As I spoke, the interpreters translated my testimony to everyone in attendance.

If God said it, God could make it so.

Follow God; He will lead you in the right way. Be open to the opportunity that God will give you, because He can see what you cannot.

Blessed is the man who trusts in the Lord, and whose hope is the Lord. (Jeremiah 17:7 NKJV)

Just as He did for me, God has given each of us a vision to fulfill. Some of us keep putting it off. The saddest part of it all is that many have died, or will die, having never stepped out on faith or put their trust in God.

Instead, you let your doubts, fears, and lack of faith take over. You have allowed family members and friends to talk you out of the dream God has placed inside of you.

Remember what the Lord has already done in the past; that should give you the faith of what He will do.

Stop worrying about what people say and focus on what God can do. Allow Him to lead you into the unfamiliar.

Do not be afraid. Why? Because God wants you to trust Him more. Faith is your foundation. It is not too late to make a fresh start with God.

Now faith is the substance of things hoped for, the evidence of things not see. (Hebrews 11:1 NKJV)

God requires your willingness, obedience, and faith. Stop making excuses about the things you have or do not have in order to do what God asks. Whatever you require, God will provide.

Remember, it is not about you, but about God. We must be willing to sacrifice all for God. We must be willing to serve God by speaking and sharing our testimonies of what God has done for us—how He saved us and made us complete again. He forgave us and kept us covered in His blood when we were living in our sin, yet God never stopped loving us.

Someone somewhere is waiting to hear from you. Trust God. Pray and ask Him to help and guide you. He is waiting for you.

For the eyes of the Lord are on the righteous, and His ears are open to their prayers. (1 Peter 3:12 NKJV)

Remember, God is all that you need.

CHAPTER SEVEN

From the Valley to the Mountaintop

The way to the mountaintop is through the valley. I praise God for my valley experience because, had I not gone through the valley, there is no way God would have placed my feet on top of the mountain.

This mission, journey, and assignment God has given me to fulfill as He opens more doors for me to speak is something God has molded me to do.

Regardless of where God leads me or to whom God directs me speak, and even when the tears begin to flow as I share my testimony of His greatness—even when I feel the nervous knots and fire in my belly, I will speak because I know that God is standing with me no matter what stage or platform I am on.

I am so grateful to God. I can never thank Him enough for where He has brought me. He continues to open doors to places I never imagined my voice would be heard, to bring awareness to groups of people who have the power through God to bring about change in the ugliness of sexual abuse and human trafficking.

Yet, there I was reading an email I received from Bill Woolf, director of the Human Trafficking Program at U.S. Department of Justice in Washington D.C. Bill asked if I was available to sit on a panel on January 14, 2020, which was also going to be televised on CSPAN.

The topic was "Summit of Combating Human Trafficking." Besides myself, there was another Survivor Lead who would be on the panel. We would be answering questions posed to us from the United States Attorney General for the District of Minnesota, Erica MacDonald.

Talk about being nervous. One of my colleagues even shared the live stream link to everyone in the division where I worked. My first thought was whatever they didn't already know about me from reading my book *Mute But Now I Speak*, they were going to find out on this day.

I wasn't sure how I would be received when I returned to the office, but I was pleasantly surprised. I received so much support and respect, and so many hugs and thank-yous for my bravery and courage to speak up. Another colleague even asked me the question, "So when are you going to run for office?"

"My response was, "What office?" and they responded, "Congress," then turned and walked away.

That thought never crossed my mind. However, it did bring forth a memory of a text message I received from Rev. Andra Hoxie in December 2012 about the United States House of Representatives. Even then, my response was, "I do not see it."

Yet, God not only opened the door for me to speak at the Department of Justice in January, but also for an interview with Jenn Pellegrino, White House Correspondent for One America News Network in Washington, D.C. on March 6, 2020.

The words to the below song by Kurt Carr and the Kurt Carr Singers are exactly how I feel.

"I've got so much to thank God for

So many wonderful blessings

And so many open doors

A brand new mercy

Along with each new day

That's why I praise you and for this I give You Praise.

For every mountain You brought me over

For every trial you've seen me through

For every blessing...Hallelujah, for this I give You Praise."

For those of you who are sitting on your dreams and not fulfilling the purpose that God has birthed inside of you, it is time for it to manifest; it is time for you to be a blessing to someone else and receive the blessings God has for you.

It is time to release the pain you have been holding onto and let the process of healing begin so that you can walk in your purpose. Every painful, negative thing that has ever happened to you or me is now in the past. No matter how you may have started, you can finish strong.

> *"Life is an adventure with mountains, valleys, and roadblocks. And we never know how to fit; we are to navigate them all until we have to.*
>
> *No matter how far from home we are or how distant the goal, with a steady pace, patience, and perseverance, we will arrive. All God's children have traveling shoes. Venture forth; the bridge will be there."*

—Susan L. Taylor, Former Editorial Director at *Essence Magazine*, July 2003.

My final thought and prayer for anyone going through a valley experience is to put your hands in God's hands. He will do the same for you as He did for me: lift you up from the pit of the valley.

To God be all the glory for the great work He will do in you and through you.

God's blessings be on you always!

Notes

Psalm 23:3-4; 32.1; 3:3; 32:1; 28:6 (NKJV)

Psalm 32:5 (NKJV), Psalm 116:1-2 (NLT), Psalm 18:19 (NIV)

Psalm 37:23-24; 40:1-3 (NLT), Psalm 50:15 (NKJV)

Psalm 73:28 (NKJV), Psalm 62:8 (NLT)

Isaiah 43:19 (NIV), Isaiah 61:1-3 (NKJV)

1 Timothy 1:15-16 (NLT)

2 Timothy 1:7 (NKJV)

John 8:7 (NLT), John 8:12 (NKJV)

Matthew 7:1-3 NKJV), Matthew 6:34 (NLT)

Hebrews 13:5 (NKJV), Hebrews 13:21 (NLT), Hebrews 11:1 (NKJV)

Proverbs 3:5-6 (KJV)

Job 22:28 (NIV)

Jude 2 (NLT)

Jeremiah 29:11; 1:5 (NLT), Jeremiah 17:7 (NKJV)

2 Corinthians 12:9 (NLT)

Philippians 4:13 (KJV), Philippians 4:19 (NLT)

Proverbs 16:9 (NLT)

Luke 1:37 (NLT)

Habakkuk 2:2 (NKJV)

Acts 10:13-15 (NKJV)

1 Chronicles 4:10 (NKJV)

1 Peter 3:12 (NKJV)

References

Webster's New World College Dictionary, Fourth Edition

SELAH Devotional "Find Your Purpose" – 05/15/20

New Life Church – www.newlifect.com

Tears of A Clown by Smokey Robinson & The Miracles, released December 12, 1970 https://www.history.com/this-day-in-history/tears-of-a-clown-gives-smokey-robinson-the-miracles-their-first-1-pop-hit-finally; **"The Tears of a Clown Album."** *Lyrics.com.* STANDS4 LLC, 2020. Web. 7 Jul 2020 <https://www.lyrics.com/album/67487/The-Tears-of-a-Clown>

Karen Ward Founder of Personality Speaking www.blog-talkradio.com/personalityspeaking

The Butterfly Effect – How Your Life Matters– Author: Andy Andrews – Published: 1998 – Publisher: Thomas Nelson www.andyandrews.com/ms/the-butterfly-effect

My Beautiful Broken Shell – Words Of Hope to Refresh the Soul – Author: Carol Hamblet Adams – Published: 1998 – www.carolhamletadams.com

For Every Mountain released in 1997 by Kurt Carr & The Kurt Carr Singers

Susan L. Taylor, Former Editorial Director at *Essence Magazine*, July 2003.

CPSIA information can be obtained
at www.ICGtesting.com
Printed in the USA
LVHW090253210821
695734LV00004B/507

9 781632 211927